# EAT DESSERT FIRST

DESIGN:  MARK EIMER

## WRITTEN BY:

Chris Brethwaite,
Cheryl Gaines,
Bill Gray,
Allyson Jones,
Kevin Kinzer,
Mark Oatman,
Dan Taylor,
and
Myra Zirkle.

EASTER 1954

Give
yourself a
gold star
for everything
you do today.

# Dot

all your " i's "
with smiley
# FACES.

# Sing
### into your
### hairbrush.

# Grow a milk mustache.

# Smile
## back at the
## man in the
# moon.

# Read
## the funnies.
## Throw the
## rest of the
# paper
# away.

# Dunk
# YOUR
# COOKIES.

# Ask
## somebody
# if their
## refrigerator
# is running.

JUL 53

# PLAY
## A GAME
### where you
### make up
### the rules
as you go along.

Order with
**eyes**
that are
**bigger**
than your
stomach.

**Open** a pack of **cupcakes** and give one to **a friend** even though you **wanted both** of them for **yourself.**

# STEP
## carefully
# OVER
## sidewalk
# CRACKS.

# Change into some play clothes.

Try to get
someone
to trade you a
# better
sandwich.

# Have a
## staring contest
# with your
# CAT.

# Eat
## ice cream
## for breakfast.

# Kiss
## a frog,
### just in case.

# Blow
## the wrapper
## off a straw.

# Refuse to eat crusts.

# Ask
## "why?" a lot.

# Make
### graham-cracker-and-frosting sandwiches.

# Believe
in a
## fairy
## tale.

JAN 63

# Have
## someone
# read
## you a story.

# Eat
## dessert
# first.

# Wear
your favorite
# shirt
with your favorite
# pants
even if they don't
# MATCH.

# Sneak
### some frosting off
# a cake.

# Refuse
to back down in a
## "did vs. did-not"
# argument.

# DO A
## cartwheel.

# Get

someone
to buy you
something
you don't really

# need.

MAY 1958

# Hide
### your vegetables
## under YOUR
# napkin.

# Stay up past your bedtime.

# Make a
## "slurpy" sound
### with your straw
## when you get
### to the bottom of a
# milkshake.

# Sit

really still
for as long as
**the dog**
is asleep
in your lap.

JULY 1957

# Put
way too much
## sugar
## on your
## cereal.

# Play a song you like really Loud, over and over.

# Find
## some pretty
# stones
## and save them.

Let the
STRING
all the way
out on your
kite.

# Stick
## Your head out
### the car window and
# moo
## if you see a
# cow.

# Walk
## barefoot
## in wet
## grass.

# Giggle
## at nude
## statues
#### in a museum.

# Make cool screeching noises every time you turn a corner.

# Count
## the colors in a
# rainbow.

# Fuss
## a little,
### then take a
# nap.

JUL 53

**Take**
a running
**JUMP**
over a big
**puddle.**

# Eat
## dinner
### at the coffee
## table.

# Giggle
## a lot for no
# REAL
## reason.

# Make
## a clover chain
## for someone
## for someone
## you really
## "like-like."

# Stir
## ice-cream
# flavors
# together.

# Do that
tap-someone-on-
the-shoulder-while-
you-stand-on-their-
opposite-side-and-
they-turn-around-
and-no-one's-there
# thing.

# Enjoy
### Your all-time
# favorite
### candy bar.
### (Remember,
### you've never heard
### of calories!)

# Wear
## a ball cap
## backwards.

# Go to the ZOO.

SAY
"duh"
when stuff is
obvious.

# Throw
### something
#### and when it lands
### make a cool
# exploding
# bomb
# noise.

# Put an orange slice in your mouth, peel side out, and smile at people.

Try to
EAT
all the
chocolate
off a peanut
butter cup.

Every time
someone says
"See you later"
SAY
"Not if I see you first"
or "Thanks for the
warning" then
LAUGH
real hard.

SEP · 59

**Whistle**
the theme from your
**favorite**
**TV show**
**all day.**

# HELP
your salt-and-pepper
## shakers
# TALK
to each other
in high, squeaky
# VOICES.

# Remember
## to say your
# prayers.

# Squish
## some mud
### between your
# TOES.

MAY • 69

**Stay up**
late watching
**SCARY**
**MOVIES.**

# BUY
## yourself a
## helium
## balloon.

# Ride
## a roller coaster
# two times
# in a row.

# SING THE
## "I See London,
## I See France"
song to someone

wearing low-slung

# pants.

# Eat
## peanut butter
## straight out of
# the jar.

When your
# GUM
starts losing
## its flavor,
## spit it out
## and get a
## new piece.

AUG 1957

# WRITE YOUR sweetie's initials in a chalk heart on the sidewalk.

# Wave
# to the
# engineer.

# Make a SMILEY FACE with your bacon and eggs.

# Run
## through the
# sprinkler
## with all your
# clothes on.

# Lick
all the ice cream
## OUT OF AN
## ICE CREAM
### sandwich
before you eat
the sandwich
# PART.

# LOOK
## down
### as you walk
### and hope to find
## money.

APR • 59

# Catch
## lightning
## bugs in a jar
## and make a
# lantern.

# Practice
## whistling
### through your
# teeth.

# EAT
## cereal
### any ol' time
### of the day
#### you feel like it.

# Yell out
"opposite day!"
### then tell someone
## they're really
# smart.

# Wear a bubble gum MACHINE RING.

# Watch
## a lot of TV
## and don't feel
# GUILTY
## about it.

# Skip a stone across A POND.

# Make
## somebody
### laugh just when
### they start to
# drink
## something.

MAY 1957

Eat just the chocolate **STRIPE** out of your Neapolitan ice cream.

# Ask
## TO BE
### excused.

# Chew
## bubble
# gum.

# SPIN
the stem of
# AN APPLE
to see what letter
it comes out on.